30 Days on:
Total Transformation

30 Days on: Total Transformation

a journal companion

Pr. sean lumsden

NoOffSwitichPress

Spokane, Washington

© 2017 by Sean Lumsden

All rights reserved. No part of this publication may be reproduced, stored in a retrieval system, or transmitted in any form or by any means, electronic, mechanical, photocopying, recording or otherwise, without prior permission of the publisher.

This book is available for bulk sales, promotions, premiums or fundraisers. Please contact the publisher at NoOffSwitch@Outlook.com for more information.

Abide in Me, and I in you. As the branch cannot bear fruit of itself unless it abides in the vine, so neither can you unless you abide in Me. I am the vine, you are the branches; he who abides in Me and I in him, he bears much fruit,

John 15.4

Contents

Day 1: Agreeing with our Identity?	8
Day 2: A New Creation	10
Day 3: The Incarnation	12
Day 4: A MUST Mentality	14
Day 5: Repentance	16
Day 6: Baptism in the Holy Spirit	18
Day 7: Receiving the Baptism in the Holy Spirit	20
Day 8: Jesus' Baptism	22
Day 9: Temptation #1, Physical Needs	24
Day 10: Temptation #2, Jesus and _____	26
Day 11: Temptation #3, Catch me God!	28
Day 12: Jesus and Power	30
Day 13: Jesus' First Sermon	32
Day 14: Jesus and Authority	34
Day 15: Authority to Heal	36
Day 16: Prepared for Impact	38
Day 17: Powered by Prayer	40
Day 18: The Faith of Friends	42
Day 19: The Faith of Friends pt. 2; Power of Forgiveness	44
Day 20: A Tax Collector and Friends	46

Day 21: Fasting	48
Day 22: Transformation	50
Day 23: Lord of the Sabbath	52
Day 24: Stretch Out Your Hand	54
Day 25: All Night Prayer, Disciples and Reverse Healing	56
Day 26: Beatitudes	58
Day 27: Love Your Enemies	60
Day 28: Give and it Will Be Given	62
Day 29: Pupil and the Teacher	64
Day 30: Good Tree, Good Fruit	66
Bonus Day 31: Build Upon the Rock	68
Appendix 1: Why Journal	70
Appendix 2: Picking a Bible	72
Appendix 3: Agreements	74
About the Author	78

Hi.

You hold in your hand a journal companion.

This booklet is designed to make journaling a deeply transformative time. Each entry will tackle a different subject. As you take a month of your life to study these subjects you will find your mind will grow. As you journal on each entry you will find your spirit and emotions will grow as well.

Transformation is a process of stopping the bad **and** starting the good.

If you stop the bad **or** start the good, you grow. To truly be transformed you have to do both. If I want to improve my financial world I can either cut expenses **or** raise income. If I do both at the same time my financial world gets better very quickly.

This booklet looks at the Life of Jesus in the first six chapters of Luke and usually adds in a passage from Paul.

The great news is if you are a Christian you ALREADY have all of Jesus. Transformation is the process of Jesus getting all of you.

I am thrilled you've taken your faith seriously enough to start this process. Everything in Christianity comes down to seeking the Kingdom first. Journaling makes your invisible world visible, and the intangible voice of God working in you as tangible as pen and paper.

You won't regret it.

Pr. sean lumsden

Day 1, Agreeing with our Identity

John 15.7 If you abide in Me, and My words abide in you, ask whatever you wish, and it will be done for you.

Romans 12.2 Do not be conformed to this world, but be transformed by the renewing of your mind.

The verses above sum up the Christian experience.

Our hope is that our human mind is renewed to the truth of who we are in Christ. This will ensure that His life, love and power flow purely and powerfully through us to our world.

Until my mind is renewed, my need, greed and demand for acceptance flows through me.

Transformation sounds something like this:

To the degree
I agree
With my identity
Is the degree
I walk in victory
Embody His glory and
Enforce His authority.

Look at the last three lines; isn't this what we hope for in our faith?

Walking in victory over sin and circumstances. Embodying the undefeatable glory promised to us since we have 'Christ in us.' Seeing the authority of Jesus come crashing into the impossibilities of life.

All of these things are already in our Spirit. We just have to agree with the truth of His word over our emotions.

Yes, it takes faith to agree with the Bible...but we already have faith. We just habitually place our faith in our senses as opposed to the Spirit. So that is what this booklet is about; learning to agree with our identity and becoming transformed into Jesus-ishness.

When I started exercising again, my mind knew I had to start getting in better shape. Sadly, my emotions and body disagreed with my mind. Over time, I found playing tennis was a fun way to stay in shape, so my emotions started to agree with my mind. My knees, however had an entirely different opinion. Eventually, I started to feel better physically and exercise became a blessing instead of a reason to contemplate suicide.

Now, my body still gets sore, and new aches and pains pop up all the time. But, my life has been transformed because I chose to agree in action with the *best of me* instead of the *laziest part of me*.

The same is true in the Spirit. When we choose to apply our faith in what the Bible says over what our emotions say we become transformed into WHO WE REALLY ARE!

You have Jesus in you and around you. Now let's learn how to agree with the reality of salvation.

I AM in Jesus and Jesus is in me.

What areas of my life are easier to agree with Jesus in me and what areas are more difficult?

Day 2, A New Creation

Luke 1. 30 You will conceive in your womb and bear a son, and you shall name Him Jesus. He will be great and will be called the Son of the Most High... The Holy Spirit will come upon you, and the power of the Most High will overshadow you.

2 Cor 5. 17 Therefore if anyone is in Christ, he is a new creature; the old things passed away; behold, new things have come.

Just as Jesus was the first of a new creation...so we become a new creation when we are in Christ.

Jesus was fully God and fully man. When He was born, He was fully God yet still lived in a fully human body. Mary was told by the angel that she was going to become impregnated by the Holy Spirit. When the Spirit came upon her, her egg was fertilized by the power of God, so the child that resulted was the Son of God. Still fully human, but instead of being born with a human spirit, He was born as the second person of the Trinity.

When we become a Christian, our human spirit is united to the Holy Spirit and we become a new creation. Just as a human egg ceases to exist when the egg is fertilized, so our old 'self' is gone. This is why Jesus and Paul called this transformation the 'new birth.' At the moment of conversion, you have all the DNA of Jesus in your spirit. You are as saved as you will ever be. Your future now becomes one of growing into WHO YOU ARE.

When a baby is born, they have all the DNA they will ever have. They also have all the muscles they are ever going to have. What they choose to do with those muscles is up to them. They can eat right and exercise and make the most out of the DNA they have. Or...they can do what I have done most of my life; eat as I want and exercise by getting off the couch and looking for the remote.

The same is true in your spiritual life. Upon salvation, you are a new creation. When God looks at you He sees you IN Christ and Christ IN you. Your old self is gone.

This is what your faith is about; learning to agree with the real, eternal you while ignoring the lies of the enemy that are telling you that you haven't changed. We may have habits still kicking around in our flesh, but we need to appreciate that those old forces of our past are dead. They may pretend to be alive but Jesus killed them on the cross.

Now, any sinful impulses are coming from the outside in. They might feel like they are inside you, but the Bible teaches that the deepest part of ourselves is our spirit. Our spirit is filled with the Holy Spirit. Sin comes from outside and tries to get inside.

I AM a new creation. Old things are gone and ALL things are being made new!

Do you have a habit or two that you have seen fade away since you became a believer? Do you have a habit that you know will fade away soon?

Day 3, The Incarnation

Luke 1.11 For today in the city of David there has been born for you a Savior, who is Christ the Lord.

2 Cor. 5.19 God was in Christ reconciling the world to Himself ... and He has committed to us the word of reconciliation...we are ambassadors for Christ, as though God were making an appeal through us.

Jesus represented God to the world. We represent Jesus to our world. We are the incarnation: round two.

If you want to know what God is like, look at Jesus. He lived completely convinced that He was God in human flesh.

His statements "I and the Father are one (John 10.30)" or "If you have seen Me you have seen the Father (John 14.9)" make it perfectly clear Jesus was God and knew He was God.

Jesus came to earth to show mankind what God was like and how humans are to act and treat each other. If you have taught someone how to accomplish a task, you may have said: "let me do it and you watch me." This is what Jesus' incarnation was...God saying, "watch me and copy this."

Paul said that we now participate in the same work that Jesus accomplished. Jesus appealed to man to be reconciled to God and now we appeal to our loved ones to be reconciled to God.

Essentially our job is to say to those around us "if you want to know what Jesus is like...look at me."

OK...take a breath...that isn't as scary as it seems.

Remember, you have the very same life in You that Jesus had. The same power that raised Jesus from the dead now lives in us. We may still wrestle with trusting the power of our emotions but that doesn't change who we really are in Jesus.

Jesus' ultimate example of God was when He willingly died on the cross. As He was being murdered, He prayed for the forgiveness of those murdering Him, so He could live for all eternity with His murderers. Jesus showed us that love and power look like self-sacrifice.

Our job is to love those around us with the same self-sacrificing service. In America, we judge success by how many people are serving us. In the kingdom, we judge success by how stinky the feet are that we have the privilege to wash.

So, what does this mean for your identity? It means your job isn't to live climbing the ladder of success. In Jesus, we are as secure and significant as we can be. Nothing can take us out of God's hands, and we were given the same assignment that Jesus was given.

I AM Jesus' representative to my world.

How does knowing we are Jesus' representative change how you see your time and your life?

Day 4, A MUST Mentality

Luke 2. 43 The Boy Jesus lingered behind in Jerusalem. And Joseph and His mother did not know it... So when they saw Him, they were amazed; and His mother said to Him, "Son, why have You done this to us? Look, Your father and I have sought You anxiously." And He said to them, "Why did you seek Me? Did you not know that I must be about My Father's business?"

Phil 3.12 Not that I have already obtained it or have already become perfect, but I press on so that I may lay hold of that for which also I was laid hold of by Christ Jesus. Brethren, I do not regard myself as having laid hold of it yet; but one thing I do: forgetting what lies behind and reaching forward to what lies ahead, I press on toward the goal for the prize of the upward call of God in Christ Jesus.

We only have one picture of God as a teenager. That sounds funny...

Luke only gives us one glimpse into the preparation of Jesus before He is baptized and launched into His ministry.

Joseph and Mary had travelled to Jerusalem with all their family and friends as was their custom. The huge caravan made their way to the festival and started back home. Suddenly, they realize Jesus is missing. Technically they were a day's walk away...but that rush of adrenaline when you realize you've lost something is always a 'suddenly' moment.

Now, I have had a prolific career as a 'loser.' I've lost almost everything you can imagine. But Mary and Joseph lost God. That's a tough one to top.

When they return, they search all over the city before they ever think of going back to the temple. Before we get critical, how many of us would look for a teenage boy in church?

When they find Him, they see Him deep in conversation with the teachers. His response gives us a clear look into His priorities. "Didn't you know I must be about my Father's business?" If there is one thing I would give every child that comes through my church, it would be that 'must' spirit.

As a believer, we have the heart and mind of Jesus inside of us. Every morning we can wake up convinced of our purpose…we MUST be about our Father's business. When Jesus told us to 'Seek first' the Kingdom, He made this conclusion in the middle of talking about worrying. Remember, seeking suffocates worrying.

America will tell us we MUST be about everything except Kingdom building. But if we can refocus on what Jesus focused on, I believe we will walk into a greater anointing and impact than we ever have experienced.

For a believer, there should never be any boredom. If we fully grasp who we are in Jesus we can know every conversation and interaction is a possibility to show that we are about our Father's business.

I AM focused on my Father's business.

If your next breakthrough were contingent on being about Kingdom business, what would change tomorrow?

Day 5, Repentance

Luke 3.2 John... came...preaching a baptism of repentance for the forgiveness of sins... "You brood of vipers, who warned you to flee from the wrath to come?

Eph. 2.8 For by grace you have been saved through faith...not as a result of works...we are His workmanship, created in Christ Jesus for good works

Let's give it up for John the Baptist ladies and gentlemen...or should I say you brood of vipers...

I'm surprised we don't have more songs celebrating our viperness...

John articulates our need to be forgiven before God. Repentance is how we do this.

Jesus came to the earth to die; to shed His perfect blood to cover our sin. Now Jesus' death accomplished more than just payment for our sins, but for today lets focus on this.

God had to punish sin since He is just. But, since Jesus WAS God, His death became the means of our justification. Therefore, Paul can write that God was both Just and Justifier in the third chapter of Romans.

When someone comes to Jesus and has faith that His sacrifice has made us right before God they become 'saved.' This is why Paul writes in the verse above that we are saved by faith and not our own good works.

But let's clarify something: whenever Paul talks about works, he is referring to works of the Law. Every Jew had to accomplish the right 'works' to be acceptable to God. Paul tells us that Jesus' works are what make us saved.

Note though- we are still created to do good works. Paul writes that we are God's work of art designed to share His love and life to those around us.

My favorite analogy is that we all are like a priceless painting that has faded with age. On top of the faded colors, other people have spray painted hateful words on top. Words like 'loser' or 'stupid.'

Our job in becoming Christ-like is to discern which words have been spray painted on top and remove them by applying the word of God.

When we repent, we rethink. Repentance is more about your future than your past. In the past, you may have felt stupid, but now you can rethink and realize Jesus has forgiven you and now, you can walk in the mind of Christ.

For the believer, repentance is our greatest joy. We can always rethink and find the mind of Jesus.

I AM God's work of art, created for the work of God.

Do you still have hateful words that are seared on your brain? What is the opposite truth from the word of God about who you are?

Day 6, Baptism in the Holy Spirit

Luke 3.16 As for me, I baptize you with water; but One is coming who is mightier than I, and I am not fit to untie the thong of His sandals; He will baptize you with the Holy Spirit and fire.

Acts 19.4 Paul said, 'John's baptism was a baptism of repentance...When Paul placed his hands on them, the Holy Spirit came on them, and they spoke in tongue and prophesied.'

Matt 28.19 Go therefore and make disciples of all the nations, baptizing them in the name of the Father and the Son and the Holy Spirit, teaching them to observe all that I commanded you; and lo, I am with you always, even to the end of the age.

We have agreement...John the Baptist, Jesus, Peter, Ananias and Paul ALL agree: Jesus baptizes believers in the Holy Spirit.

We said yesterday, that when someone repents and puts their faith in Jesus for salvation they become a new creation; the Holy Spirit is united with their human spirit. We call that conversion, regeneration or being 'born again.'

But we see in this story in Acts that regeneration is only the first step; to walk in the fullness of Christ-like-ness, believers need to be baptized in the Holy Spirit.

Imagine Christmas day and your kids run downstairs at the crack of dawn. But instead of tearing open the gifts like a pack of wild wolves, they simply sit next to them and leave them unopened. This is like believers who accept Jesus as their savior, but don't pursue baptism in the Spirit. The gifts are there...they just remain unopened.

Please note- this isn't an issue of salvation, but empowerment. Upon salvation, the Holy Spirit moves in...but until the Baptism of the Spirit, the power, direction, wisdom and impact remain unencountered.

Jesus saves us because He loves us. Jesus baptizes us in the Spirit because He loves everyone around us. Our job as believers is to show our world how much Jesus loves them in both our actions as well as by bringing the power of God crashing into the impossibilities of their lives. Jesus showed us 'this is what God looks like.' After Spirit baptism, we show our world 'this is what Jesus looks like.'

At the Great Commission, Jesus tells His disciples these things: Make disciples as you go! The command is to make disciples, not merely converts.

Then Jesus tells us what that looks like: baptizing them in the name of the Father (repentance) , the Son (receiving Jesus) and the HOLY SPIRIT. After His ascension, He will tell His disciples they are not ready to accomplish their task until they 'receive power (Acts 1.8).' That is what the Baptism of the Holy Spirit is about: The capacity for supernatural impact.

Tomorrow we will look at how to receive the baptism and how a prayer language fits into that reality.

I AM Ready for ALL the Holy Spirit has for me!

If you could envision a greater life of spiritual empowerment, what would that look like?

Day 7, Receiving the Baptism in the Holy Spirit

Rom. 8.26 In the same way the Spirit also helps our weakness; for we do not know how to pray as we should, but the Spirit Himself intercedes for us with groanings too deep for words; and He who searches the hearts knows what the mind of the Spirit is, because He intercedes for the saints according to the will of God.

Rom 14.2 For one who speaks in a tongue does not speak to men but to God; for no one understands, but in his spirit he speaks mysteries. …One who speaks in a tongue edifies himself;… Now I wish that you all spoke in tongues, but even more that you would prophesy.

Here is the good news: Jesus loves to give His followers the Holy Spirit! In John, Jesus likens the giving of the Holy Spirit to a father feeding His children.

So…if you've never been baptized in the Holy Spirit, ask Jesus to do so. Set aside some time to worship and stay in that moment of gratitude and prayer. Start speaking your praise to God out-loud. Your tongue is the gateway to a changed life. When you speak your prayer's and worship out-loud you release the Spirit inside you.

After some time, you will start to sense the life of Jesus rising up.

Now go and share that love with people. The Baptism of the Spirit is contingent on using this empowerment to bring people closer to God. You must use this power or it goes dormant. BUT- the more you pour out, the stronger you get.

Think of a dam that creates electricity. As the power of the water goes over the turbine, electricity is created. Power of the water goes over the dam, power of electricity is created and stored to be used later. That is how the Holy Spirit works in and through us. As you give out to others, you retain power for later use. If the water just stays behind the dam it gets stagnant. And I think we all would agree we have too many 'stagnant' Christians.

Another analogy is a military soldier. A warrior becomes a warrior by the training they receive and the battles they engage in. When we are filled with the Spirit we get stronger internally as we fight spiritual battles. Every warrior becomes more effective the more they fight and train.

You may also ask another Christian to lay hands on you to receive the baptism of the Spirit.

Now let's talk about how a prayer language ties into the baptism of the Holy Spirit. Please remember, a prayer language is not the baptism in the Spirit. The baptism can release a prayer language but a prayer language and Holy Spirit baptism are not the same thing.

A prayer language is a personal communication between you and God. This language both builds you up and enables you to pray the perfect will of God anytime you need to. My entire faith is built around the hour or two I pray in my prayer language every day. My praying in my prayer language is a complete mystery…yet God uses this to release His wisdom and will into my mind. Therefore, Paul says 'I pray in tongues more than all of you' and 'I pray with the Spirit and pray with understanding.'

The bottom line is this; if you want to minister like Jesus you need to release all that Jesus has placed inside of you. And that is why the baptism of the Holy Spirit is essential to your faith.

I AM an empowered vessel of the Holy Spirit

Why don't you use this time to be baptized with the Spirit or ask to be re-filled with the Spirit.

Day 8, Jesus' Baptism

Luke 3.21 When ...Jesus was ...baptized, ...heaven was opened, and the Holy Spirit descended upon Him in bodily form like a dove, and a voice came out of heaven, "You are My beloved Son, in You I am well-pleased."

Eph 3.18 To know the love of Christ which surpasses knowledge, that you may be filled up to all the fullness of God.

Do you see identity in Jesus' baptism? Look how God the Father spoke of Him: Jesus was God's son. Jesus was loved. God was 'well-pleased' with Jesus.

Isn't that what we strive to hear from our earthly parents and loved ones?

From the position of being a loved son who has pleased His Father, Jesus walked into and out of the temptation period without failing.

Note how in Ephesians, Paul makes the statement that as we understand Jesus' love we become filled with the fullness of God. If you ask me, that is quite a statement...we can be filled with the fullness of God.

Why is knowing God's love so important? Because when we understand how secure we are in God's protective hands we can take the risks He asks us to. We can risk loving a tough person knowing they might not love us back.

When we understand how significant we are in God's heart and plan, we can willingly serve and love like Jesus did. I can self-sacrificially love whomever is in front of me without any expectation of them returning the favor.

When we love another person with the expectation that they will give us what we need, we stop loving them and start manipulating them. Its only when we know how much we are loved by Jesus that we can stop using people as our drug.

Until then, we can't be empty enough of our own neediness to be truly 'filled with the fullness of God.'

Jesus, after His baptism, didn't have His intelligence confirmed. He didn't have His anointing confirmed. He had His identity as a loved Son confirmed.

When we become a disciple, we become 'in Christ' and He lives in us. This means the love that God has for Jesus is now ours. When that radical fact goes from head knowledge to heart knowledge you can start to live 'filled with the fullness of God.'

So why do we struggle with this knowledge? First, it seems too good to be true. And…it is (that's called grace). Second, the enemy is committed to programming people to trust everything BUT God for our future. We've heard that lie in our head for so long we believe that voice is our own.

This is why agreeing with your identity is so important. If you need people's approval to function…they become your god. But when you live with the confidence that you are God's beloved child in whom He is well pleased, you can live empowered to change your world.

I AM a loved Child of a God and He is proud of me!

What part of the three affirmations (son, loved, pleased) is easiest and hardest to believe about you?

Day 9, Temptation #1: Physical Needs

Luke 4.1 Jesus, full of the Holy Spirit...was led around by the Spirit in the wilderness for forty days, being tempted by the devil. And He ate nothing during those days, ... He became hungry. And the devil said to Him, "If You are the Son of God, tell this stone to become bread." And Jesus answered him, "It is written, 'MAN SHALL NOT LIVE ON BREAD ALONE.'"

Phil 4.19 God will supply all your needs according to His riches in glory in Christ Jesus.

Right after Jesus was baptized and had His identity affirmed, the devil tempted Jesus about that identity.

The first thing to note about this passage is that Jesus was led by the Spirit into the temptation. To prepare for this, Jesus chose to fast to ensure He was spiritually prepared for the confrontation.

Fasting is how we tell our flesh 'NO!' Fasting teaches your body that your spirit needs to be in control. Essentially, fasting is a type of silent, all-day prayer.

Since Jesus was hungry, the devil seized on that opportunity to tempt Him usuing every human's biggest fear; not getting our physical needs met.

Jesus turned this temptation on its head by telling the tempter that spiritual hunger is far more important than physical hunger. This is akin to when Jesus said if we "seek first the kingdom that all these things (physical needs) will be given to us (Matt. 6.33)."

Paul also reminds the church that God will meet our needs based on Jesus' grace. Remember; this verse follows Paul thanking the church for their sacrificial financial gift.

Do you see a pattern here?

The devil starts his attack on Jesus' identity (If you are the Son of God) and then implies that Jesus could easily turn a stone into bread if He just uses His power for His own needs.

Don't we face that same temptation? "If you were really loved by God, He'd give you more expendable money to tithe from and not expect you to be sacrificial..." I know I've heard that.

Note Jesus' and Paul's responses; Spiritual Hunger is the bedrock of seeing all of God's intervention. Jesus will say 'to the measure YOU give it will be given back. Paul will say 'those who sow sparingly will reap sparingly.' God puts the power of sowing and reaping in OUR hands.

Note this: the greatest gift God can give is spiritual hunger.

One time when I was broke and whiny I threw myself an epic pity party. After patiently listening, I sensed God say, "I want to bless you but you haven't sown any seeds for me to bless." Ouch.

So, what keeps us from giving or sowing abundantly? A combination of two forces; forgetting the goodness of God and forgetting how much God loves His children.

(That's us by the way...this is a booklet on identity...)

Jesus fought His flesh with a fast and fought the devil with the Word. Can we do the same?

I AM driven and fed by God's work in my world.

What is harder for you to have faith in; God's goodness or how much He loves you? Have you ever risked and seen God bless you in an area of need?

Day 10, Temptation #2: Jesus and _____

Luke 4.6 The devil said to Him, "I will give You all this domain...; for it has been handed over to me, and I give it to whomever I wish. Therefore if You worship before me, it shall all be Yours." Jesus answered him, "It is written, 'YOU SHALL WORSHIP THE LORD YOUR GOD AND SERVE HIM ONLY.'"

Rom 1.1 Paul, a bond-servant of Christ Jesus, called as an apostle, set apart for the gospel of God

The first temptation questioned whether God would provide for physical needs. This temptation questions whether TOTAL devotion to God is the only option.

Satan may be a liar, but that doesn't mean everything he says is a lie. Every temptation is like a fishing lure; a small bit of bait that is the truth. But that small truth is wrapped around a big, sharp, hook-shaped lie.

The truth in this temptation is that Satan was given domain over this planet when he stole it from Adam and Eve. I liken this to me giving my car keys to my son who then sells them to a drunk driver. My intention was for the car to be used by my son and not Drinky-McDrinkface. The drunk driver would be responsible for what he did with my car as would my son. I would only have responsibility to the extent that I trusted my son.

Satan could have given Jesus a kingdom without that pesky cross. Note- Jesus didn't disagree with that element of Satan's authority.

All Jesus would have to do is worship before the devil. Jesus could still worship God; He just needed to have Satan also on His side.

You see this fact stressed in how Jesus answers: 'worship God ONLY.'

American Christians have a tough time with this; we love to worship 'Jesus and...'

Jesus and: Money, lust, fame, power, drugs, porn, gambling, apathy, rage, fear, quitting, stress, inactivity, hyper-activity, eating etc etc.

Was your pocket sin on the list? I have a few.

I believe what keeps us from our destiny is usually our 'Jesus and ____.'

This is why Paul found his identity in being a slave of Jesus. Single-hearted devotion is the beginning of walking in the power of God. Jesus has a beatitude that reads 'blessed are the pure (focused) in heart for they will see God.'

We all, like Jesus, need to carry our single-hearted devotion up our hill while we carry our cross. Satan offered Jesus a cross-less kingdom. Sadly, many Christians live a cross-less Christianity.

We love the thought of heaven and a nice place to go on Sunday once a month if the Seahawks aren't playing. The heart of our faith is that God on a cross shows us what love looks like and expects us to replicate that servant's heart.

It makes me wonder if Jesus would believe anyone's Christianity can be cross-less. His wasn't.

I AM solely empowered by serving like Jesus.

Name three things that would make your 'Jesus and ___' list. Think how you can change and then burn the list if you want.

Day 11, Temptation #3, Catch me God!

Luke 4.9 And he led Him to Jerusalem and had Him stand on the pinnacle of the temple, and said to Him, "If You are the Son of God, throw Yourself down from here; for it is written; 'HE WILL COMMAND HIS ANGELS CONCERNING YOU TO GUARD YOU,' and, 'ON their HANDS THEY WILL BEAR YOU UP, SO THAT YOU WILL NOT STRIKE YOUR FOOT AGAINST A STONE.'" And Jesus answered ... "It is said, 'YOU SHALL NOT PUT THE LORD YOUR GOD TO THE TEST.'"

Satan can quote scripture...just not well.

How you handle temptation is vital. All of your best decisions came because you resisted temptation. All your worst decisions came because ...well you know the rest.

The first temptation said; 'don't do anything until your physical needs are met!' The second temptation said; 'I can do most things with Jesus' blessings but I need help from other sources. This temptation says; I can do anything I want because God will protect me from myself. To this Jesus says: Don't tempt God.

Let's look at this from two angles. The first is that Satan always tempts us towards self-destruction. Jesus was promised a cross-less kingdom if He acted self-destructively.

Every addiction has an element of self-destruction because when we choose self-rule over being ruled by God we move away from the eternal life Jesus gives us.

The second angle is about expecting God to protect us when we do something aggressively against His will.

Jesus' kingdom required Jesus' death on the cross. Satan offered Jesus a flashy, crowd gathering option. "Go and jump off the temple and watch the angles catch you and the crowd run to you! You'll surely become the king and won't have to die to get there!"

If you would have given me that option, I'd be sprinting toward the edge! "Catch me God!!" This temptation has two things I love; crowd's cheering me and no pain. Add in pizza and you'd have my trifecta.

Sadly, every Christian knows that if we make destructive choices God frequently will let us learn the hard way. Sow stupidity, reap wisdom. Painful wisdom.

So how do we learn from this temptation? First, know self-sacrifice is essential to a life of faith. There are no prestigious feet to wash. The smellier, more drug-injected the fee are, the better.

Second, be assured there will be steps of faith, just be sure God is behind them. God is OK with people asking like Peter; "Lord IF IT BE YOU, ask me to walk on the water."

How do we know if its God and not our flesh? Simple- seek first his Kingdom and not our comfort.

I also must add, every believer who has ever made an impact has misheard God's voice in a decision or two. God wants us to worship Him and not success. Failure is impossible if your goal is only to become more like Jesus. God works all things together for good FOR THOSE WHO love God and are called according to HIS purpose.

I AM led by God's plan everyday!

When have I jumped into something that might not have been God's best?

Day 12, Jesus and Power

Luke 4. 14 And Jesus returned to Galilee in the power of the Spirit, and news about Him spread through all the surrounding district.

1 Thess 1.5 for our gospel did not come to you in word only, but also in power and in the Holy Spirit

Did you notice Luke's progression? Mary would be overshadowed and the power of the Holy Spirit came upon her at the conception of Jesus.

John sums up Jesus' ministry with the Baptism of the Holy Spirit.

Jesus' baptism has the Holy Spirit descend and rest upon Him.

The temptation narrative describes Jesus as being 'full of the Spirit.'

And after Jesus defeats the Devil, He is 'in the power of the Spirit.'

I think Luke is trying to make a point about the power of the Holy Spirit in Jesus' ministry…

Paul on multiple times makes the same case about His ministry like the verse listed above.

Christianity in a nutshell is agreeing with Jesus in our beliefs and behavior. You cannot agree with Jesus in your behavior if you don't have the working of the Spirit in your life. We call this working of the Spirit the gifts of the Spirit. We will talk about those later.

For now, let me clear-up how we read the stories of Jesus.

When you first start to read the Jesus stories, it is easy to walk away feeling like the person who was touched by Jesus and had their life changed. We were once lost and Jesus found us and so we share in that gratitude.

As you grow in your faith, you may feel like the disciples. You relate with wanting to love Jesus, but still feeling trapped in your selfish ways. You know what it is like to have one great moment and the next moment stick your foot in your mouth.

These are all legitimate Bible study perspectives. But...

The person we are to emulate is Jesus! Our goal is to do what Jesus did! You as a believer have the same Holy Spirit inside that raised Jesus from the dead. The people healed by Jesus or the disciples in the stories do not. You can still learn from them as a believer, but your goal is to become like Jesus.

When you see Jesus stop to heal a blind man while the people in the temple are trying to kill Him, you can learn to look beyond your personal priorities.

When you see Jesus washing the disciples feet, you can stop looking up the corporate ladder and look down to find dirty feet to wash.

And when you find religious people picking on a person trapped in sin, you can show both the religious and the seeker that love always seeks to bring people closer to God, love does not attack them for being far from God.

Oh yeah...and go pick up your cross and follow Him.

Luke will keep talking about the power of the Spirit when we get to his book called Acts. Only in Acts 2, the power comes into us.

I AM a vessel of the Holy Spirit's power.

Who can I love like Jesus tomorrow?

Day 13, Jesus' First Sermon

Luke 4.14 And He came to Nazareth ... He entered the synagogue on the Sabbath, and stood up to read... : "THE SPIRIT OF THE LORD IS UPON ME, ... HE ANOINTED ME TO PREACH THE GOSPEL TO THE POOR.... TO PROCLAIM RELEASE TO THE CAPTIVES, AND RECOVERY OF SIGHT TO THE BLIND, TO SET FREE THOSE WHO ARE OPPRESSED, TO PROCLAIM THE FAVORABLE YEAR OF THE LORD." ...Today this Scripture has been fulfilled in your hearing."

I Cor 5. 18 Now all these things are from God, who reconciled us to Himself through Christ and gave us the ministry of reconciliation.

It's on. Jesus is in his home town where the people have been gossiping about Him and His birth since He was born. Now though, He is a travelling Rabbi ready to make a statement.

The reading for the day was out of Isaiah 61. Jesus quotes this prophecy about the Messiah that was to come. Then He does two shocking things.

First, He doesn't finish the passage. Jesus stops at 'favorable year of the Lord' and doesn't complete the thought. He leaves out the Jewish people's favorite element; 'the day of vengeance for our God.'

If that isn't shocking enough, Jesus then says to all the people that had made His childhood years a living hell that HE is that promised Messiah.

Friends, if Jesus wasn't the Messiah, he was a liar. If Jesus wasn't God in a bod, he was crazy. Either way, if these two statements aren't true...he deserved to be stoned or crucified for blasphemy.

But what if they were true? I believe they were.

In this moment, Jesus tells everyone He was the promised messiah and that this will be an era of God's favor towards men. People will very soon be able to walk into God's presence because of what Jesus was about to accomplish. God's vengeance will soon come upon Jesus on the cross, to give people the opportunity to live without any fear of judgment from God.

What does this mean for us and our identity? We are God's ambassadors of love and possible redemption to our world. This IS the crux of our identity as we've discussed earlier.

The second implication is that we are bringing a message of reconciliation between God and man. Right after Paul calls believers new creations, he tells us that we further the work of reconciliation between God and man.

So, if you are a new creation, then you are a minister of God's reconciliation to your world.

I AM God's agent of reconciliation.

Who in your world is far from God and how can you make a kingdom impact today?

Day 14, Jesus and Authority

Luke 4.31 He was teaching them on the Sabbath; and they were amazed at His teaching, for His message was with authority. In the synagogue, there was a man possessed by the spirit of an unclean demon, and he cried out with a loud voice, "Let us alone! What business do we have with each other, Jesus of Nazareth? Have You come to destroy us? I know who You are—the Holy One of God!" But Jesus rebuked him, saying, "Be quiet and come out of him!" ... he came out of him without doing him any harm.

2 Cor. 10.4 for the weapons of our warfare are not of the flesh, but divinely powerful for the destruction of fortresses.

Authority is the core issue of the Bible. God gave Adam authority to rule and Adam gave that to Satan. Jesus invaded the earth as a man to take back that authority so He could entrust the authority to His disciples.

Jesus is again teaching in a synagogue. This group is amazed by the authority His teaching holds. They aren't the only ones amazed at Him; some demons showed up to see what all the fuss was about. When they arrived, they recognized Jesus from before the earth was created. You can tell by their response; they are terrified their time of judgment has come.

Did you notice Jesus' priority? He was more concerned with the person than the spectacle. We see here a central aspect of Jesus' work; He sees every oppressed person as a prisoner of war.

You'll notice Jesus didn't inquire as to the sin in the man's life that might have caused the demonic infestation. He didn't ask about generational sins. He didn't make the person confess his sins. Jesus just acted like a police officer- the demon was hurting the person and had to go.

Paul in this quote clearly teaches that we are in the midst of a spiritual battle. As such, we need to learn how to use the spiritual weapons we have been given.

Jesus took back all authority when He rose again. Since we are 'in Him' and He is 'in us' we share the same authority to see people delivered from tormenting spirits.

How do we do this? We simply stand in our authority and speak to the spirit like Jesus did. Luke 10.19 tells disciples they have authority over the enemy's ability.

Think of it like this; the badge of a police officer gives them the authority to stop traffic or arrest someone. We have the 'badge' of Jesus' authority, to set people free or heal in His name. In both instances, the authority is conferred based on position. The policeman is positioned as an extension of the laws of the city. We are positioned as an extension of Jesus' power and authority. The legal system backs up the policeman. Jesus' power backs up the disciple.

Demonic activity is not behind every problem we face. However, the devil will add discouragement and doubt to every problem we face.

We will discuss this more as we go on, but for now, we must have faith that Jesus has given us power over all the enemy's ability (Luke 10.19). The more we agree with our identity as Jesus' deputies, the greater results we will see in getting people set free.

Remember, we don't have authority over people, just the abilities of demonic powers as long as we have faith in our identity.

I AM the instigator of Divine Intervention!

How does this explanation of deliverance similar to or different from what you have learned before?

Day 15, Authority to Heal

Luke 4.38 Now Simon's mother-in-law was suffering from a high fever...He rebuked the fever, and it left her;...While the sun was setting, all those who had any who were sick with various diseases brought them to Him; and laying His hands on each one of them, He was healing them.

1 Cor 12.8 For to one is given...to another, gifts of healing by the one Spirit.

In yesterday's entry we saw Jesus use His authority to cast out demonic spirits. Today we see Him heal by the same authority.

Everywhere Jesus went He did three things: teach, heal and deliver. When He sent the disciples out to other cities, He told them to do what He had been doing; teaching, healing and delivering. This is Jesus' method of bringing Kingdom power into the lives of people.

Note in this story, Jesus 'rebuked' the fever like it was a demon. This doesn't mean that all sicknesses are demonically directed, but in this case Jesus discerned that was the case. On one level, all sickness comes from the door of sickness and death that was opened by Adam and Eve. But not every sickness and disease comes from demonic forces.

Once again, we see Jesus not concerning Himself with anything except delivering the suffering person.

Some people in the church believe physical healing is up to God's will. I believe that Jesus' stripes bought our healing as recorded in Isaiah 53; 'by His stripes we were healed.' The issue isn't whether it's God's will to heal, but whether we carry enough authority to see the healing fully come to pass.

Jesus is always on the side of 'abundant life' where the thief has sowed theft, death and destruction. Jesus had 100% results when it came to physical healing. Our job is to always be growing in our agreement with Jesus, which will increase our impact. As usual, disciples must agree with the word over our emotions and experiences.

When we minister healing, we are sowing life where the devil has already sowed ***and reaped*** sickness. Some healings happen instantly and that builds our faith. Some healings take time and that builds our faith and character.

I have read almost every book on healing, and every person that has had success seeing people healed has attributed their growing success rate to making a practice to pray for every person, every time. Almost unanimously, they all agree that the more they pray the greater their results are.

The other issue in growing in healing effectiveness is growing in character. Sadly, many Pentecostals have wanted power more than have wanted to agree with Jesus by growing in integrity.

I believe this process is the renewing of your mind. This happens when the truth of God goes from our heads to our lives. It's not enough to know the truth; we must apply the truth. Jesus says in Mark 16:18 that His followers will lay hands on the sick and they will recover. Our job is to now choose to agree with Jesus and minister healing to all we come across.

I AM empowered to bring healing!

Have you ever heard of someone being healed after being prayed for?

Day 16, Prepared for Impact

Luke 5.5 Simon answered and said, "Master, we worked hard all night and caught nothing, but I will do as You say and let down the nets." When they had done this, they enclosed a great quantity of fish, and their nets began to break...And Jesus said to Simon, "Do not fear, from now on you will be catching men."

Eph. 3.20 Now to Him who is able to do far more abundantly beyond all that we ask or think, according to the power that works within us, to Him be the glory in the church.

Are you ready to make an impact?

This is a great story; the life-long fishermen have been out all night without catching anything. Jesus tells them to cast out on the other side. Simon is quick to tell Jesus of their past success, or lack thereof, when he catches himself: "But I will do as you say."

When Simon throws his nets to the other side, the catch is bigger than they can hold. All night working with their best information brought nothing. Obeying Jesus brought the catch of a lifetime.

Every one of us could tell the story of a lifetime of effort that has made us more tired and broke than ever. We probably have rehearsed many excuses for our lack of productivity.

Yet Jesus still comes to us and asks us to believe and obey again. Jesus always has another kingdom option we haven't thought of yet.

Paul writes in Ephesians that God wants to do even more in our lives than we can ask or think. I can personally think of some amazing things I'd love to see God accomplish.

After Paul writes this he clarifies that the greatness God wants to do is based on the power of the Holy Spirit inside of us. So how do we access this power?

Two steps; inward and out-word. First, make sure you live full of the Life of Christ. This requires taking in God's word through reading, listening to sermons, reading and discussing with other believers. Then, make it a habit to share what you have learned, or pray for someone every day.

Paul considers 'renewing of our mind' the cornerstone of being transformed into Christ-like-ness. Note that isn't merely accumulating knowledge. Its taking in the life of God and then applying that life to yourself and everyone around you. A farmer could starve while having the greatest seed collection on the planet if he never plants, waters, prunes and harvests.

I hope you see the new life Jesus wants to give us! He wants to take the pain from our past and use those experiences to transform our future. Think about it: every pain, trauma, frustration and place of death can be transformed into a powerplant of growth.

You've had enough frustration being a poorly fed fisherman! Now, let's listen to Jesus, throw our nets over the side and go fishing for the enhancement of everyone we meet.

The night's over. Futures are at stake. There are children who will grow up in healthy, love-filled homes because you are choosing to invest in their parents today.

I AM Jesus' fisherman to my world. My joy and peace is the bait and His love is the hook.

Who today needs you to bring them the life and love of Jesus? What is stopping you from doing that?

Day 17, Powered by Prayer

Luke 5.12 A man covered with leprosy; and when he saw Jesus, he fell on his face and implored Him, saying, "Lord, if You are willing, You can make me clean.'… (Jesus said) "I am willing; be cleansed." And immediately the leprosy left him… "But go and show yourself to the priest" …But Jesus Himself would often slip away to the wilderness and pray.

1 Thess 5.16 Rejoice always; pray without ceasing; in everything give thanks; for this is God's will for you in Christ Jesus. Do not quench the Spirit.

In just a few verses we read some transformative ideas.

First, the man with leprosy asked a question that many believers ask 'is God willing to heal?' Jesus answered definitively; Yes, God is willing to heal!

Every time we see Jesus come upon a sick person, Jesus heals them. You never see Jesus make someone sick so He could heal them later. You never see Jesus leave someone sick so that person's character will grow.

Jesus treats every suffering person like a prisoner-of-war and immediately sets them free. Jesus sees 100% success because He walks in 100% submission to the Father 100% of the time. As we grow in our agreement with Jesus and intimacy with the Father, we will grow in our success as well.

The second element applies to how we grow in receiving our healing. Jesus tells the healed man to go back to the priest to show them that he is healed. To us this seems like a formality.

Imagine though, that you are the healed person. This means you must go back to the place of your greatest disappointment. At some point in this man's life, it was a priest who looked at him and pronounced his life as over. He had leprosy and was condemned to social death by isolation before he suffered an excruciating death by leprosy. And Jesus says: "Go back."

For us to get healed from past wounds and stay healed we must learn to take our healing back to the place where we were hurt. We must be able to view past times of breaking as times where Jesus sustained us even when we felt He didn't protect us.

When we can do this, we stop being victims! We learn to deeply forgive where we've been deeply hurt. We place Jesus at the center of our life and dethrone our places of trauma. Just like Jesus walked Mary back to the tomb of Lazarus, so we must walk back with Jesus to our places of grief. God wants to cry with us before He brings forth new life.

The third thought is we see how Jesus stayed so spiritually powerful; He left the crowds to spend time alone with God. If Jesus had to spend large times alone with God, don't you think we need to as well?

David knew he could kill Goliath publicly because he had killed a lion and bear privately. Your public triumphs are built on your private times. We all have friends and loved ones who need us to pave their way back to God through prayer and intercession. Their lives won't change until our commitment to prayer changes.

I AM empowered to heal and I AM growing in wholeness based on my time alone in God's presence.

Do you have places where you still need more inner healing? Why don't you 'go back' in your spirit to a place of trauma and write about your healing story.

Day 18, The Faith of Friends

Luke 5.17 And the power of the Lord was with Jesus to heal the sick. Some men came carrying a paralyzed man on a mat and tried to take him into the house to lay him before Jesus. When they could not find a way to do this because of the crowd, they went up on the roof and lowered him on his mat through the tiles into the middle of the crowd, right in front of Jesus. When Jesus saw their faith, He said, "Friend, your sins are forgiven."

This is a very important story that we will break into two days.

The previous story was about healing and so is this. Only this time we have a different expression of faith.

In the previous story the leper crossed social bounds in his desperation and only had one concern; is Jesus willing to heal. That was answered quickly when Jesus said: "I am willing." Here though...we see nothing from the paralyzed man.

We do see extreme faith from his friends. First they knew Jesus could heal him so they took the initiative. They picked him up and carried him to the feet of Jesus.

When we pray, we bring our loved ones to the feet of Jesus. They may not be ready or able to engage Jesus on their own, but our faith can initiate a divine intervention. Never underestimate the power of prayer to bring our loved ones to Jesus.

Next, we see them taking extreme measures. They don't just bring him to Jesus, they destroy every hindrance in their path. In case, they destroyed a perfectly functional roof.

Are we that desperate? Are we willing to destroy our perfectly acceptable TV viewing schedule to pray? Or are we willing to destroy our perfectly acceptable wake up time to pray?

Are we willing to be seen as 'a little crazy' by those around us in our effort to bring our world under His Kingdom authority?

I am becoming more convinced that until we are looked at as being 'a little crazy' by other Christians we will not see the breakthroughs we are contending for.

Everything WILL bow its knee at the name of Jesus. Our job is to make them bow NOW and not just at the end of time.

But we must agree and align with our identity as the carriers of kingdom breakthroughs. We initiate Divine intervention and will tear off a perfectly functional roof if we must. Our loved ones may have to ride on our faith until they can walk to Jesus on their own.

We have all the faith there is, but usually we must take our faith from the **visible** circumstances and place it onto the **invisible** power of the Holy Spirit in us. Every person has faith in their emotions...that faith must move to faith in Jesus.

I AM the carrier of faith for my world. And if need be, I will carry my friends and tear off roofs!

Who in your life may need a little extra time in prayer or service to get to Jesus?

Day 19, Faith of Friends pt 2; Power of Forgiveness

Luke 5.21 The Pharisees ... began thinking to themselves, "Who is this fellow who speaks blasphemy? Who can forgive sins but God alone? Jesus knew what they were thinking and asked... Which is easier: to say, 'Your sins are forgiven,' or to say, 'Get up and walk'? But I want you to know that the Son of Man has authority on earth to forgive sins." So he said to the paralyzed man, "I tell you, get up, take your mat and go home."

2 Cor. 7.10 For the sorrow that is according to the will of God produces a repentance without regret, leading to salvation, but the sorrow of the world produces death.

Three points to consider.

First, the Pharisees interpret this instance as Jesus claiming to be God. Here is one of the clearest instances in Luke of Jesus' self-knowledge as being God. Note the power of His ENEMIES interpreting this and not just Jesus saying this.

The central point of Christianity is Jesus is God. Only Christianity says that God became a man. If you want to know what God is like; look at Jesus. And here it's His enemies making this connection.

Second, Jesus is Son of God, Son of David, Suffering Servant and Son of Man. Son of Man is the prophetic name for the Messiah being the final judge for sin. When Jesus tells the parable of the 'Sheep and the Goats' in Matthew 25, He calls Himself the Son of Man.

The religious leaders understand that, but since He likened the Son of Man to forgiveness of sins, He was saying that the Son of Man would also be divine.

And of course, Jesus heals the man to show both the power to forgive and give life. Two things only God can do.

Our meditation thought for today was the power of forgiveness. The paralyzed man's friends were sure his biggest need was physical. Jesus shows here that our biggest need is spiritual. Our physical problems can make life a living hell. Our spiritual problem called sin will make eternity hell.

Sin is not just a passive problem because it is so pervasive in life. Sin is saying to God I don't need you. Sin is choosing to be your own god. Ultimately, sin dims the light of God's life.

Almost every Sunday, I walk over to the horizontal blinds on the windows of our sanctuary. I show people how a life of agreement with Jesus is like the blinds fully open and allowing the light to shine into the room. Then I go the other direction and show the effects of sin in our lives. The light is always there... we just have to open our lives with agreement and let the light in.

Jesus shows us that being forgiven is the greatest power on earth. In the next breath, Jesus heals the man, backing up His claim to be God. Jesus frequently healed and then would say 'this is what the Kingdom looks like...lives forgiven and empowered to do the same!'

Too many American believers are content with just being forgiven. The forgiveness of sins is certainly the path to new life, but it's ONLY the path! We must travel that path into our destiny. Moving into your identity means embracing the fact that sin-less-ness should lead us into a life of powerfulness.

I AM pure before God so God's power can flow purely through me.

Are there patterns or habits that are keeping you from walking in the full power of God?

Day 20, A Tax Collector and Friends

Luke 5.21 Jesus went out and saw a tax collector... Levi. "Follow me," Jesus said...Levi got up, followed him...Levi held a great banquet for Jesus at his house, and a large crowd of tax collectors and others were eating with them. But the Pharisees complained..." Why do you eat and drink with tax collectors and sinners?" Jesus answered... "It is not the healthy who need a doctor, but the sick."

1 Cor 9.22 I have become all things to all men, so that I may by all means save some.

What a picture...Jesus at a party with the worst of the worst.

We have no one in American society that is as hated as the tax collector. The Jewish tax collector would buy this position from the Roman government. He then would have the backing of the Roman soldiers to collect any amount of money from his Jewish neighbors. Rome didn't care how much he kept for himself as long as they received their share. Most tax collectors were the wealthiest people because of their systematic theft.

So, the fact that Jesus would talk to a tax collector let alone call one to come be a disciple, was offensive to the Jewish people beyond belief.

But when people see an offence, Jesus sees a person. Levi got up from his desk and started following Jesus.

Levi was so amazed at the transformation Jesus made that he threw a party and invited all of his friends to meet Jesus. Here is where we see the Pharisees again being upset with Jesus.

Can you imagine Jesus, overhearing the discussion, turning and giving His answer? I'll bet you could have heard a pin drop.

Here we see God's heart perfectly personified. God's heart is for those who are spiritually sick. For those who don't have it all together, who don't get invited to the right parties. To Jesus, if you've been rejected by men you'll be accepted by Me.

Sadly, too many American Christians have removed themselves from the messy lives of their friends from their pre-Christian days. When we do that, we align ourselves with the people who will eventually crucify Christ.

We all rub elbows with people who need Jesus. We are God's point of access into their lives. When we choose to only socialize with believers, we limit God's reach into our world. Yes, God can reach them without you…but His plan is to reach them through you.

I understand that sometimes new believers must break away to stay sober or make new attachments. That is healthy. But for those of us who have been disciples for a while, we need to hear God's heart for the lost and be His access point.

I AM God's bridge into the lives of those I love.

Who in your world needs more of your time to help build a bridge for God's activity?

Day 21, Fasting

Luke 5.33 Jesus was asked "John's disciples often fast and pray, and so do the disciples of the Pharisees, but yours go on eating and drinking." Jesus answered, "... But the time will come when the bridegroom will be taken from them; in those days they will fast."

Jesus says fasting should be a part of His disciple's spiritual life. Fasting is a great spiritual discipline because we learn how to live while our flesh is being denied.

Fasting teaches your body that it doesn't get everything it wants. Hunger won't kill you. Fasting will teach your body that your spirit needs to be in control.

Fast as you can, not as you can't. Fasting isn't a hunger strike; God isn't being pressured to answer a prayer because I skip breakfast.

Fasting is a type of silent, all-day prayer. When you start to feel uncomfortable you are saying 'no' to the good (eating) so you can say 'yes' to the great (getting a spiritual breakthrough).

What do you want more? Your comfort zone or a spiritual breakthrough? You will get whichever you desire most.

Some people may see fasting as a form of legalism. I can't imagine Jesus suggesting we do anything legalistic. Paul also fasted.

There is a difference between fasting because you want to be more like Jesus and fasting because you feel you must fast to please Jesus. Jesus IS pleased with you. Fasting is just learning to thin your flesh so more of Jesus' life flows through you.

We must hold these two thoughts in tension: we worship our Father God because He is God regardless of what we see in our life. AND our Father God wants to explode into our circumstances and bring His power and authority to see His kingdom come and

His will be done. They are not contradictions; they are a plumb line that must be held tightly to maintain the straight edge for us to walk along.

Remember, the most important part of fasting and prayer is the PRAYING! Make sure you take extra time away from lesser activities and put that time toward a kingdom breakthrough.

Fasting is a Jesus approved method to bringing His kingdom here on earth. Our call is to hunger and thirst for righteousness… and fasting is a great way to bring that into your life.

I AM capable of starving my flesh to strengthen my spirit through fasting.

Could you skip a meal a day? Could you fast unhealthy food items and go pray instead? Is there something besides food you can fast? TV is a great place to start.

Day 22, Transformation

Luke 5.36 No one tears a piece out of a new garment to patch an old one. Otherwise, they will have torn the new garment, and the patch from the new will not match the old. And no one pours new wine into old wineskins. Otherwise, the new wine will burst the skins; ... No, new wine must be poured into new wineskins.

Rom 8.5 For those who are according to the flesh set their minds on the things of the flesh, but those who are according to the Spirit, the things of the Spirit. For the mind set on the flesh is death, but the mind set on the Spirit is life and peace,

In one parable, Jesus answers the two thoughts that plague people the most; how do we fix broken things and change bad situations into good ones. And His answer is the same to both; don't simply fix the bad, create something new.

For the first thought, we see a picture of needing to fix the functionality of something that was broken. If a garment has a hole, body parts are peeking through and cold air is getting in.

Maybe in your world, you have a habit that is sucking the life out of your life. Maybe self-sabotage is turning into self-destruction.

For the second thought, Jesus uses the transformation process as the example. Wineskins were intended to stretch once with the transformation of water into wine. If you tried to use the skins twice, they would be destroyed. So how do we apply these?

Maybe in your world, you've started down a path of learning to become Jesus-ish and you feel you've stalled in your growth.

The answer for the two, Jesus states, is that you can't use a new piece of cloth to fix an old garment and you can't put new wine in old wineskins.

New life requires new thinking. The old, torn ineffective garment needs to be replaced with the new garment. The new wine, needs to be transformed in a new wineskin.

Life in Jesus is never meant to be an improvement of the old but instead a radical replacement into a new way of thinking and living.

The me-first mind has to be replaced with a kingdom-first mind. The comfort-now mind has to be replaced with kingdom -now mind.

And the great news: Paul says the new mind of the Spirit is already in us... we just need to set our mind and actions on living in agreement with what is true.

The elite athlete makes hundreds of choices every day that will align their commitment to health or performance. This becomes more than a statement of preferences but a radical reordering of your life behind your identity.

Best of all, Jesus tells us that when we become Kingdom focused, all of the things we need in this life will be provided. We just need to learn to seek with our mind and actions and not just our good intentions.

I AM living out of my new thinking and not my old neediness!

What areas in your life need a kingdom tune-up? Your time? Your best efforts? Your finances? What is keeping you back?

Day 23, Lord of the Sabbath

Luke 6.1 … on a Sabbath…His disciples were picking the heads of grain…the Pharisees said, "Why do you do what is not lawful on the Sabbath?" And He was saying to them, "The Son of Man is Lord of the Sabbath.

Gal. 4.9 How is it that you turn back again to the weak and worthless elemental things, to which you desire to be enslaved all over again? You observe days and months and seasons and years.

What should a believer's relationship be with the Sabbath and how does it affect our identity?

The great irony is I started this entry on a Saturday which is my Sabbath. As I did my research, I felt that gentle nudge of the Holy Spirit asking if this project was 'work?' I sighed, shut my laptop and went off to do my Sabbath activities.

So how should believers observe the Sabbath? I would say both religiously and non-religiously. How's that for clear?

I'll work backwards. We should not celebrate the Sabbath out of a religious obligation. First, we should not observe the Sabbath out of guilt, fear, or obligation. Sabbath is a joy that is given to us by God to ensure our lives stay in balance with Him as our highest priority.

But we should celebrate the Sabbath 'religiously' if we mean regularly.

Everything in our faith hinges on seeking the Kingdom first. Jesus should receive the best of our time, talents and money. We should give because we love Jesus and that love is seen in obedience.

For the Sabbath, we see that Jesus is always doing good on the Sabbath. He goes out of His way to show the Pharisees that the day of rest is meant to be celebrated by participating in the activity of God. Activities like healing people, teaching people and setting them free from the bonds of the evil one.

How should we celebrate the Sabbath? The same way! There is no question, our Sabbath life should involve spending time with fellow believers, worshipping together, teaching Sunday School, shaking hands with new people, and praying for others. These are the activities that re-invest in us what we invest in others. This is time and life invested…not spent. Remember, Jesus said 'the measure that YOU give YOU will receive.'

Personally, since I work on Sundays, my Saturday Sabbath is about praying, journaling, reading or listening to smarter people than me, taking worship walks with my dog or spending prayer time in my prayer hot tub.

Yes, I go to the gym, sit in the hot tub and pray… its my favorite prayer closet. The shower works well also.

The bottom line is that we need to have faith that as we make Kingdom life a time priority, God will bless the rest of our time. Sowing and reaping are placed in our hands…Sabbath investment is one of the best places we can put this into place.

I am not an exercise addict. I only run when something bigger is chasing me or I've been called to dinner. When I fell in love with playing tennis, my whole attitude changed. Now I see playing tennis as being the highlight of my week. I will go to the gym on days I'm not playing so I can exercise to play tennis better. Accordingly, my stamina is increased and I've lost weight. Anyone see where I am going with this?

Everything changes when devotional activities become a 'get-to' instead of a 'have-to.' Entertainment becomes empowerment and recreation becomes re-Creation.

I AM a person who invests time in Sabbath life, because that empowers the rest of the time in my life.

How do you celebrate the Sabbath?

Day 24, Stretch Out Your Hand

Luke 6. 6 On another Sabbath He entered the synagogue and was teaching; and there was a man there whose right hand was withered. The...Pharisees were watching Him closely to see if He healed on the Sabbath... And Jesus said to them, "...is it lawful to do good or to do harm on the Sabbath, to save a life or to destroy it?"..."Stretch out your hand!" And he did so; and his hand was restored.

There are a couple of great points here.

First, do you see how Jesus is trying to force the Sabbath issue? Right in the middle of church with everyone watching, this man's arm became the sermon Illustration.

The Pharisees were against any work being done on the Sabbath to make sure the day was kept holy. Jesus was committed to showing them that showing compassion and the power of God is how believers in God are to keep the day Holy!

This is why serving in church is such a great way to spend your Sabbath. When we invest our lives in making disciples, we are doing the work of God. When we invest our lives in making our church a stronger place, we become a stronger people.

This is an important point- yes you can and should volunteer doing good charitable work. But that isn't the same as investing in your local church. When you serve at church, you have the prophetic opportunity to practice your spiritual gifts on another believer in a safe environment so that when you go out and share your faith outside of church, you have experience.

If you are teaching Sunday school, some little child will ask you a tough question and you will go 'HELP GOD!' Sunday is the safe environment we have to practice on one another so when we go into the world we have good experiences under our belt.

The second point I want to make in this story is to hone in on how the man was healed. Note, Jesus didn't even touch the man...He only spoke to the man and told him to do something he couldn't do before.

Often, Jesus will see us living with a 'withered' part of our spiritual or emotional life. This man undoubtedly was marked by what he couldn't do because of his withered limb. We all have things in our life that we feel are withered. Maybe it's an addictive habit, anger or apathy.

Let me be Jesus to you… stretch out your hand! Don't wait another minute. Get up and get the help you need. Stop being marked by limitations and start being marked by the miraculous power of God!

This whole booklet is about becoming who Jesus says we are. Jesus saw that man as being whole even when the man saw himself as being broken. Jesus sees you as being whole even if your whole life has been a series of let-downs and heart-breaks.

Claim your identity as a healed, whole, Spirit-filled, empowered follower of Jesus…because that is who you are!

If you are afraid to 'stretch out your hand' like Jesus asks then celebrate that you are on the right path! You already have faith in your eyes…now have faith in the eyes of your spirit.

You ARE a new, healed, empowered, envigored, life-filled, Spirit-filled, redeemed bearer of the presence of Jesus.

Now- stretch out your hand!

I AM healed, filled, and empowered to walk out the life Jesus has poured in!

What is the withered part of your life Jesus wants to heal? What would 'stretching out your hand' look like?

Day 25, All night prayer, Disciples and Reverse Healing

Luke 6.12 He went off to the mountain to pray, and He spent the whole night in prayer...And when day came...He...named apostles... And all the people were trying to touch Him, for power was coming from Him and healing them all.

This story is an amazing look into Jesus' priorities.

Jesus used to pray all night. Think about that. We as humans love to sleep. I love to sleep so much that when I am asleep, I dream about napping.

But Jesus saw the evening- which was the Hebrew beginning of a day- as the time to pray.

Why did Jesus spend so much time in prayer? Because He needed it. Yes, He was God, but He also was as much a man as we are. He had a flesh to fight and a devil to defeat. He knew that for Him to 'only do what He saw the Father doing (John 5.19)' He had to stay united with the Father. Jesus never did one miracle through being the second person of the trinity. Every miracle came out His raw dependence on the Father.

Why do we feel we need to pray any less? Friends, the reason our lives, our nation, our family, our churches are in such disarray is because of our prayer-less-ness. The crux of Jesus' teaching is to 'Seek first the Kingdom and all these things will be added to us (Matt 6.33).' We don't seek first so all these things aren't added as much as God wants to give them and we need. The problem isn't on God's side... its on ours.

Nothing changes until our prayer life changes.

After Jesus spent all night in prayer, He was able to discern God's will for whom should be His apostles. When we spend quantity time with God we are able to make quality decisions.

Then look what happened...the crowds came to Him. When we are truly marked by the anointing of God, our mission and destiny will just come into every interaction of every day. We can stop saying 'God what is your will for my life' and just love the people in front of us.

Finally, notice the reverse power of God in this story... the people needing healing or deliverance touched Jesus and they were healed. Normally, Jesus had to touch the people or speak to the situation. Now, if people show the initiative, the healing power of God is available to everyone!

This is the picture of the preferred future God has for all of us! We pray, we make good decisions, we go about our life, and everyone who has access to us has access to all the healing they need!

Jesus said in John that out of our belly's will flow rivers of living water. God's plan is to create an army of 'living water' franchises to stroll the planet quenching the thirst of dying people who are trapped in the drought-filled, disease- infested prison ruled by the devil!

And where does this power start, flow and become increased? In your prayer closet. Not your entertainment closet. Not your comfort closet. Not your pity-party closet. God's plan is for each believer to turn entertainment into empowerment, a pity-party into a power-party, and a drive for comfort into a drive for conquest.

What if your next breakthrough, or the next breakthrough of a loved one depended on your prayer life?

Guess what...it does.

I AM empowered to be God's answer to life's problems.

How much victory do you want and do your loved ones need?

Day 26 Beatitudes

Luke 6.20 Blessed are you who are poor, for yours is the kingdom of God. Blessed are you who hunger now, for you shall be satisfied. Blessed are you who weep now, for you shall laugh.

Rom 12.1 Therefore I urge you, brethren, by the mercies of God, to present your bodies a living and holy sacrifice, acceptable to God, which is your spiritual service of worship.

Luke's version of the beatitudes is different than Matthew's. While Matthew fixes on the spiritual attitude of a kingdom follower, Luke seeks to stress the radical nature of kingdom life against the expected promises of a Jewish believer.

First, we have to understand the concept of 'blessed.' In Greek thought, every skill a person held was a 'blessing' from a god. For example, if you were a fast runner, you were said to be 'blessed' by Mercury. If you were strong, you were 'blessed' by Heracles. So we must understand- the blessing of God is Godliness. This blessing is to be used for influence, not affluence. American Christians link being blessed to being comfortable. Jesus links blessing to being a person of kingdom influence through service.

We see this in how Jesus shares the beatitudes in Luke. The words linked to 'blessedness' are the opposite of what a Jewish person would expect from God.

'Poor…Hungry…Weeping…Hated.' The prevailing belief was that if you are in God's covenant with Israel, that your life would be marked by wealth, fullness and happiness. But Jesus turns that belief on its head in verse 24 when He says 'but WOE to your who are rich…and well fed.'

WHAT??? Being rich, well-fed and happy are what Americans pursue constantly? How are we going to build a big church teaching this??

Jesus is drawing a line of demarcation; Kingdom living is a radical departure from living for your own self-fulfillment. Kingdom life is about self-sacrificial service to others.

Like the little child who yells 'the king has no clothes!' so Christ-followers need to be willing to live according to the TRUTH revealed in Jesus and not the opinion that each person's comfort zone demands.

Paul will write that human flesh is at constant odds with life in the Spirit: "For the flesh sets its desire against the Spirit, and the Spirit against the flesh (Gal 5.17, see also Rom 8.1-17)."

Jesus sees the invisible war between life and death, God and Satan, and He tells His followers that the way we win the cosmic war is to win the internal war. Set your expectations to live according to Kingdom self-sacrifice and not personal self-aggrandizement and you will truly be blessed.

American Christians want to be blessed; Jesus wants His followers to LIVE blessed. A whole life of blessedness, not just a moment. A pattern of blessing not just a lucky break. God made Solomon the wisest, richest man on earth because Solomon wanted God's best for God's people more than for personal comfort. When God sees that you want what God wants, He knows He can trust you with the world.

Remember- that is what prayer is about; Prayer is not me asking God for what I want, but God asking me TO ASK HIM for what HE wants.

Jesus is going to explain Kingdom life in the next few verses; but first He had to blow the minds of those who want to follow God for personal gain. "Woe to you when all men speak well of you (Luke 6.26)."

I AM blessed because of my Kingdom investment of service.

How does this radical rethinking of a blessed life sit with you?

Day 27, Love your Enemies

Luke 6.27 But I say to you...love your enemies, do good to those who hate you ... offer him the other (cheek) also; treat others the same way you want them to treat you...35 But love your enemies, and do good, and lend, expecting nothing in return; 36 Be merciful, just as your Father is merciful.

Hold on tight.

Right now in America, the sexual teachings of the Bible are not popular. In the rest of the world, for the past two-thousand years, these teachings from Jesus to love your enemies of Jesus have not been popular.

The radical renunciation of personal revenge may be the most radical of Jesus' precepts. Even as I write this, I want to make qualifications but I am not going to do that. Let's just look at the words of Christ and not water them down because of our own fear of exploitation.

Loving your enemies may be the most difficult attitude for a person to hold. We cry- "BUT Jesus...didn't you see what they did?"

Turning the other cheek may be the exact opposite of 'healthy boundaries.'

Lending, expecting nothing in return, is the exact opposite of the American financial system. Technically, this goes from 'lending' to 'giving.' It is quite hard to accumulate stuff if you are giving away said stuff.

And there in the midst is the central thought... 'Treat others as you would want to be treated....be merciful as your Father is merciful.'

Jesus calls us to total self-renunciation. He will eventually tell us to 'pick up our cross and follow Him.' And remember, when Jesus said this, the resurrection hadn't happened.

The other emphasis is to DO and not just respond. DO unto others as you would want them to do unto you. Don't wait! Don't play-it-safe. Don't wait to be asked. Don't wait until they 'get their stuff together.' Don't wait until they apologize. DO the right thing. DO the loving, sacrificial thing. And, DO the right thing especially if they don't deserve it. WHY? God, our Father did that for us.

If this is a bit overwhelming; Good. It means you're getting it. If you can hold on for the next entry, you'll get a better understanding. But for now, lets just sit and look our own selfishness head-on.

Our flesh demands to be in charge of our protection, provision and promotion. When we come to Jesus, He tells us to trust Him to do these three things. And when you think of it, isn't it a Father's job to protect, provide and promote their children? When I say promote, I mean teach kids how to move forward in life successfully.

And yet, Jesus points us to raw dependency on the Father. If you have problems with this type of faith, I would suggest you may not be completely convinced of the goodness of God.

Now, I will make one qualification regarding this passage. The concepts of self-renunciation for revenge is a personal position and not the position for a society. You can forgive a person who robs you. I, as your neighbor, can't overlook their crime. As your neighbor, I must act to ensure the criminal is punished and other neighbors are likewise kept safe. The sermon on the mount is not to be a crime policy nor a military policy.

But...for the individual, this is a bid to come and die to your selfishness.

I AM empowered by my self-sacrifice.

What is your reaction to living with this level of raw dependence on God's goodness?

Day 28 Give and it Will be Given

Luke 6.37 Do not judge, and you will not be judged; ... Give, and it will be given to you...For by your standard of measure it will be measured to you in return.

2 Cor 9.6 He who sows sparingly will reap sparingly.

Two thoughts including the most life-changing thought in the Bible.

First, the only verse every non-believer knows is this one: Don't Judge! You may have zero regard for Jesus, the Bible, the church or even baby Jesus in a manger, but this verse is crocheted on a pillow in your bedroom...DON'T JUDGE!

Jesus here is telling His followers not to take a superior stance regarding the person's eternal destiny. Every person is destined for hell without the blood of Jesus. This doesn't mean we approve of everything someone does, we just never write off a person based on current choices. We can DISCERN that their actions aren't healthy without judging about their eternal destiny.

Second, God has put your future in your hands.

Think about this...the sovereign God who spoke the universe into existence says to each one of His children: "Here...go plant today for what you need tomorrow."

This thought should keep you awake at night. You are standing today in the garden you've been planting your whole life.

Frequently, Christians say 'I'm just waiting on God.' This passage says God is waiting on you!

'By the measure, YOU give it will be returned.' That is Jesus talking...not TBN. Paul says the same thing when he says if we sow sparingly we will reap sparingly. One time when I was praying I asked God to bless me, and I heard Him reply 'I want to... but you haven't sown any seeds for me to bless.'

I would submit, the difference between a world-changing disciple and an American Christian is how seriously they take this verse.

Now, before someone calls this 'salvation by works' let me clarify a few things. First, this has nothing to do with salvation. We receive salvation based on the finished work of Jesus. His work is done...our work in bringing this salvation to our world is not.

Second, the grace in this passage is about sowing from Jesus' account and not mine. If you had a great investment opportunity, my bank account would have a small amount to invest. But if I had a rich uncle to back me I could invest much more. That is how it works in the Kingdom...we choose where to sow the power of God to work in our lives. I invest my small amount, and Jesus expands that with His infinite grace and power.

We sow in the direction we want to go. Do you need more time...spend more time in prayer. Do you need more empowerment...go serve more people who can't pay you back. Do you need physical healing or strength...go pray for more people. Does your marriage need help...go find some great books and sow your brain space into becoming a better spouse.

Remember at the beginning of the book: 'To the degree you agree with your identity...' All of Kingdom life starts in seed form. To the degree we take Jesus seriously in investing the power of the seed into the power of His soil is the degree we become all Jesus made us and our world comes into alignment with God's blessedness.

I AM an investor of the life of Jesus.

Where are you sowing well and where do you need to start sowing more?

Day 29, Pupil and the Teacher

Luke 6.40 A pupil is not above his teacher; but everyone, after he has been fully trained, will be like his teacher. Why do you look at the speck that is in your brother's eye, but do not notice the log that is in your own eye?

Gal 1.20 I have been crucified with Christ; and it is no longer I who live, but Christ lives in me; and the life which I now live in the flesh I live by faith in the Son of God, who loved me and gave Himself up for me.

This could be the last summation entry. 'Everyone who has been fully trained will be like his teacher...it is no longer I who live, but Christ lives in me.'

This is our goal, to fully live out our identity of being a Christian. We become the little Christ to our world.

Jesus walked on earth and said "I am what God looks like (John 14.9). We now get to walk in our world and say "I am what Jesus looks like."

Ok...that might be a stretch...but you get the idea. We represent or re-present Jesus to our world.

Being a Christian isn't about what party you vote for. Its not about what schools you send your kids to or what radio station you listen to.

It's about waking up every morning and saying 'ok...where did I put that cross.'

It's about loving your spouse like Jesus. Being willing to go the extra mile in loving and serving so that your spouse feels as loved by you as they are by Jesus.

It's about loving your children in that balance of grace and truth so they know they are loved as much as they know how to make good decisions. It's about letting your kids catch you praying and studying the word.

Its about loving your friends and family so when their life goes into crisis, you are the first person they think of to pray them into health.

It's about looking at your finances and saying how can I invest in the Kingdom and not just spend toward my comfort. For example, giving God the first ten percent so He can maximize the ninety.

It's about making recreation time, re-Creation time. Seeing prayer as a pleasure to revel in and not a duty to be endured.

It's about loving the spiritual fight. A warrior becomes a warrior through their training off the battle field as well as their time in the war. The only disciples who make a lasting impact are those who know there is a real fight and love being a part of that fight. When we get fed up with the enemy running roughshod over our loved ones, we become undefeatable as we pry the hands-of-hell off of our loved ones.

It's about living so full of God's Sprit that joy in the face of disaster becomes your calling card. You are filled with peace and you sweat peace around everyone. At some point people will look at you and say 'WOW... I bet Jesus was like that.'

And that is how your world becomes His world.

The best news? Its already in you... you just have to agree with your identity.

I AM the carrier of God's will for everyone who I contact.

What is your vision for what your world will look like as you become more like Jesus?

Day 30, Good Tree, Good Fruit

Luke 6.43 For there is no good tree which produces bad fruit, nor, on the other hand, a bad tree which produces good fruit. For each tree is known by its own fruit. For men do not gather figs from thorns, nor do they pick grapes from a briar bush. The good man out of the good treasure of his heart brings forth what is good.

Rom 8.6 For the mind set on the flesh is death, but the mind set on the Spirit is life and peace.

The journal thought for yesterday's entry was to envision what your world will look like when you become more like Jesus. Here are Jesus' and Paul's answer:

Your life becomes fruitful. Remember, these people are as focused on a fruitful harvest season as we are on having a good fiscal quarter or getting a bonus on our pay check. For them, a fruitful life meant a life of provision, options and best of all, no starvation.

So, we are to live a life of fruitfulness... but what fruit should we look for?

Are we like grapes that grow in clumps? Are we like cherries that require a tree to support the life? Are we like potatoes that grow underground connected to other potatoes? Or, are we like a watermelon, a giant fruit that takes a while to develop?

Maybe our lives are meant to be like apples that come in thousands of varieties that someone can pick and bite right into. Or maybe we are like a pineapple. A fruit that requires a very specific climate and protects our fruit in a fortress-like shell.

This is the beauty of God's Kingdom plan. Each person's fruit is a manifestation of who God created them to be.

Part of the problem though, is we live our life in jealousy of other people's fruit. Maybe we are a pomegranate and we want to be a coconut. Maybe we are a coconut that hates our hairy shell and want to be a nice juicy raspberry.

The more you become like Jesus, the more you become uniquely you. The more you conform to this world, the less unique you become.

Remember, part of a fruitful life is pruning. Pruning cuts away the dead parts of our life that are sucking the life away from the fruitful parts. If we love beautiful rose bushes in the summer, then we should love a pruned rose bush in the spring. If you can't picture that, imagine a stick, sticking out of the ground.

God wants to reproduce the best of you. To do that He has to trim away all the extra dead wood that accumulates. So remember, if you see elements of your life fall away, or people walk away, your miracle isn't in an unpruned life; your miracle will come from what is left.

And this is Jesus' promise to us…as we become more like Him we become the spring of life for all around us to draw life and strength. Best of all, we don't have to do anything but let God do His work. Our part is to learn to agree with who we really are and not panic when we lose our leaves in the winter and some extra dead wood in the spring. Harvest time is coming…and we are going to produce an abundant amount of life to share.

The Bible is a story of a fall in a garden, submission in the garden of Gethsemane, resurrection from a garden tomb and heaven being the garden of Eden revisited. Why? Because we are called to bear the fruit of love everyday of our lives.

I AM fruitful in every endeavor of my life!

What elements in your life are bearing good fruit? Where might you need some pruning?

Day 31, Build Upon the Rock

*Luke 6.46 Why do you call Me, 'Lord, Lord,' and do not do what I say? 47 Everyone who comes to Me and hears My words and acts on them, I will show you whom he is like: 48 he is like a man building a house, who **dug deep** and laid a foundation on the rock; and when a flood occurred, the torrent burst against that house and could not shake it, ...49 But the one who has heard and has not acted accordingly, is like a man who built a house on the ground without any foundation; and the torrent burst against it and immediately it collapsed, and the ruin of that house was great.*

Phil. 3.10 That I may know Him and the power of His resurrection and the fellowship of His sufferings, being conformed to His death.

This is a story believers have heard or have heard alluded to for centuries. I have preached on this for my whole career and as a youth pastor probably alluded to this story almost every week. And I just saw something new today...

Before Jesus tells this story, He links discipleship with obedience. In John 14 and 15, Jesus will link love with obedience. In the Great Commission, we will quote making disciples, baptizing in the names of the Trinity, listing the progression of cities and telling people to GO!

Yet in the middle of the commission, Jesus slips in 'teaching them to obey all I commanded.'

When did obedience become a 'legalistic' term? Jesus called obedience loving, and showed us in the way He obeyed the Father (John 14.15, 21, 23).

Here, we see two lives contrasted; one life survives the traumas of life and one life is constantly engulfed in trauma and suffering.

What does Jesus submit is the difference? Obedience.

This whole booklet is about agreeing with who you really are in Christ. As you agree in your beliefs and behaviors you will walk out all the life the Holy Spirit has poured in. The result will be that you will be the fountain of water for those with whom you interact. You will be the prophetic voice for all those who will hear. You will be the bearer of life-giving fruit to all around you. Not because of what you do as much as who you are! Fruit trees rarely pull a muscle in the fruit bearing endeavor.

All of this happens if we obey. But note one little detail: we must 'dig-down' to the rock. All the middle east is sand; the wise man 'digs-down' to the rock before building. You may have to reopen some old wounds. You WILL have to forgive those who've hurt you. You will have to put your motives under a magnifying glass. Agreeing with your identity is deeper than just mental ascent. It is a process of wrestling all those stubborn places of disagreement onto the cross every day.

But for those who do come the fruit of the spirit: love, joy, peace, patience, self-control, meekness, goodness, and gentleness (Gal. 5).

And people living with the fruit of the Spirit manifest the gifts of the Spirit: healing, prophecy, administration, admonition, teaching.

What do you say- are you ready to agree with your identity?

To the degree, you agree with your identity, is the degree you walk in victory, apply His authority and manifest His Glory.

And... walk in your destiny.

I AM all Jesus says I am.

What areas do you need to 'dig down' into? Your childhood? Your marriage? Your faith?

Appendix 1

Why Journal?

If you've never journaled, allow me to invite you into one of the greatest activities a person can get involved with.

Journaling is a spiritual discipline where each person takes their walk with Jesus seriously enough to create a tangible record. Now don't get intimidated...journaling is as easy or as complex as you wish to make it.

Journaling can be as easy as writing down a thought you read in scripture, a prayer request and something you are thankful for.

Journaling can be as complex as working through deeply held beliefs and struggles under the umbrella of prayer.

Your call. Remember, journal as you can... not as you can't.

A great starting place would be:

1. Start with being thankful for a few specific things.

2. Ask God to bring His will into specific situations on your heart.

3. Ask God to fulfill any needs you may have.

If you have some issues in your character that may need God's touch, be sure to write those down to chart how far you have come.

Next, move to writing down a thought or two from your Bible reading that day. This booklet is designed to jump start your writing with stimulating subjects. If all fails, open up to the Psalms (usually right in the middle) and read until you find a verse that echoes your thoughts for the day.

You can be specific or general in your writing. You can even use codes if you fear someone reading them. Remember, you set the rules.

The most exciting part is when you look back and see how God has answered prayer, changed your character or seen how He has spoken to you while you were processing your thoughts.

Good luck and God bless!

Appendix 2

Picking a Bible

If you don't have a Bible, here are some great things to consider.

Each Bible translation tries to bring the ancient languages into modern English. That isn't a very easy task. There are two schools of thought about the best way to approach translation.

One school of thought is that the Bible should be as easily understandable today as it was to the first people who read the text. This approach will make reading easier to understand but may take some simplifications with the interpretation. This type of translation is called 'dynamic.' These Bibles are great to read.

The other school of thought is called 'literal.' Here the translators try to bring the English to be as close to the ancient Greek or Hebrew as possible. While the translation is accurate, the English can be stilted or tougher to understand. These Bibles are great to study.

Some thoughts on modern translations:

New International Version (NIV): by far the most popular for good reason. An accurate translation that is easy to understand.

New Living Translation (NLT): Very similar to the NIV, maybe even easier to read. Great for teens.

NIrV: An NIV written for people with a lower reading level. Great for kids.

New American Standard Bible (NASB): My favorite. A Painfully accurate translation. I used to correct my Greek homework by looking in the NASB. Sadly, the English can be tough and many of the sentences are longer than they need to be. Accurate? Yes. Readable? Yes- with some effort.

English Standard Version (ESV) : Great new translation that is 97% the same as the NASB with smoother English. May be the best of all worlds.

New King James Version (NKJV): Updated King James Version. Beautiful ancient English that might be tougher to understand but wonderful use of the English language.

So- that is a quick look at the modern translation. Pick one or two and jump in!

Appendix 3

Statements of Agreement

Here is the complete list of agreements from the booklet. Say this whole list twice a day. Remember, these statements are true whether you agree or not! You might as well agree with who Jesus say you are.

I AM in Jesus and Jesus is in me.

I AM a new creation. Old things are gone and ALL things are being made new!

I AM Jesus' representative to my world.

I AM focused on my Father's business.

I AM God's work of art, created for the work of God.

I AM Ready for ALL the Holy Spirit has for me!

I AM an empowered vessel of the Holy Spirit.

I AM a loved Child of a God and He is proud of me!

I AM driven and fed by God's work in my world.

I AM solely empowered by serving like Jesus.

I AM led by God's plan every day!

I AM a vessel of the Holy Spirit's power.

I AM God's agent of reconciliation.

I AM the instigator of Divine Intervention!

I AM empowered to bring healing!

I AM Jesus' fisherman to my world. My joy and peace is the bait and His love is the hook.

I AM empowered to heal and I AM growing in wholeness based on my time alone in God's presence.

I AM the carrier of faith for my world. And if need be, I will carry my friends and tear off roofs!

I AM pure before God so God's power can flow purely through me.

I AM God's bridge into the lives of those I love.

I AM capable of starving my flesh to strengthen my spirit through fasting.

I AM living out of my new thinking and not my old neediness!

I AM a person who invests time in Sabbath life, because that empowers the rest of the time in my life.

I AM healed, filled, and empowered to walk out the life Jesus has poured in!

I AM empowered to be God's answer to life's problems.

I AM blessed because of my Kingdom investment of service.

I AM empowered by my self-sacrifice.

I AM an investor of the life of Jesus.

I AM the carrier of God's will for everyone who I contact.

I AM fruitful in every endeavor of my life!

I AM all Jesus says I am.

Other agreements:

This journal is my prophetic title deed and I will see everything written in here.
I am a kingdom seeker, a foot washer.
I lay hands on the sick and they recover.
I cast out demons with a word and they stay out.
I have an anointing that abides.
I am growing in character, growing in power, and hearing God's voice better every day.
I am preparing to do the greater words Jesus promised.
I go into all the world, and make disciple-making disciples.
I love fighting the devil, and love enforcing God's will,
I feed and am sustained by seeing God's will.

I grow stronger as I pray, longer because what God promised he can produce.
I do not grow weary in well doing, I get stronger day by day.
I know God's working for my good because I love him and am seeking his purpose.
I am a co-heir with Jesus, am seated in high places with Jesus.
Greater is the Spirit within me then is than everything in the world.
No weapon formed against me will succeed and everything that comes against me is accursed.
I am blessed by God and cannot be cursed.
I am crucified with Christ and Christ lives through me.
I am undefeatable because the life of Jesus flows through the wounds of this life.
I am a new creation, everything in me is being made new.
I am free of hurts and wounds of my past.
I am free of demonic chains.
I am free of bitterness and unforgiveness.
I am on a path that shines fuller like a sunrise.
I am a son of God and part of the bride of Christ.
I was purchased by and am perfected by the blood of Jesus.
I am filled with abundant life as I carry my cross and put my flesh of death.

About the Author

Pastor Sean Lumsden graduated from Azusa Pacific University in 1992 with a Bachelor's Degree in Theology and a Minor in Biblical Greek.

These degrees were immediately put to use as Sean started in an 18 year career as a waiter.

In 1996, Sean was licensed as a Pastor from the International Church of the Foursquare Gospel. Shortly after, he planted "jacob's ladder" one of the first 'Gen-x' churches in the nation. Not a particularly large church, their slogan was "come to jacob's ladder and get alone with God."

Eventually Sean and his family went to Spokane, Washington where Sean helped start a few churches. Additionally, he worked as a financial planner, national-award winning advertising copywriter, radio disc-jockey, music instructor and again as a waiter.

Currently, Sean is the pastor of Living Hope Foursquare, a funky little church in a funky part of Spokane. At Living Hope, their church aims to make people 'Jesus-ish'. Their slogan is 'creating Christ-like people who love people like Christ.'

Sean still writes commercials while he pastors, and in his spare time he hangs out with his family, collects musical instruments, plays tennis and takes his Saab into the shop for repairs.

This is the third book in the '30 Days on:' series. The first book was ignored worldwide. The second book was ignored both worldwide and on the Soviet space station. His mother enjoyed both books but fought Amazon over getting her money back after she read the books.

You can contact Sean at PastorSean@LivingHopeSpokane.com.